THIS BOOK IS THE PROPERTY OF

the

craft of sail

written, designed and illustrated by jan adkins

WoodenBoat
BOOKS
Brooklin, Maine

Published 2018 by WoodenBoat Books
PO Box 78, Brooklin, Maine 04616

Originally published in 1973 by
Walker Publishing Company

ISBN: 978-1-934982-17-4

Printed in Canada by Friesens

10 9 8 7 6 5 4 3 2 1

These friends are anchor and compass to me

albert bigelow
matthew finn

5

an introduction

I want to make a truthful book. I want to put in it everything a small book can hold that will help you learn about the wind and the water. I want to tell you nothing false, or misleading, or confusing; and so I will not tell you that sailing is always a fun ride with sunshine and a calm sea, nor that you can read my truthful book and know it all. Many sailors will be disappointed at not finding a single spinnaker, genoa jib, adjustable backstay, or rhumb-line computer in this book, but this is simply not a book about racing. Rather, it is a book that tries to catch in its pages the lessons a young person in the great age of sail might learn — the simple skills a waterman would use every day of a life on the water. Tactics, rules,

and advanced technology might get in the way of a new sailor feeling his way into a comfortable understanding of an old medium: wind and water.

We reside on a globe spinning in space. Photographs brought back from our voyages outward tell us that, in the way we view Mars as the Red Planet, we are the Blue Planet. The blue is our water, trimmed around by a spotty cape of white clouds riding in the thin peel of our atmosphere. Air and ocean, wind and water, two opposing elements constantly annoyed at one another. What we think of as the sea is the place where those two angry elements meet, the depth of the water below and the height of the

wind above. The wind runs along the water and furrows it, whips up waves and foam, throws it onto the beach and against the rocks. The water leaps up into the wind as spray and creeps up into it as fog. They are seldom peaceful neighbors. The only sign of peace between them is the sail-craft, a creature of both wind and water, existing in both worlds, at accord with both, using both, making a kind of bond between them, and in that bond is great power. By the wind, with the water, the sailboat somehow plugs into the basic power supply of the universe.

We forget that for most of man's history the rivers and seas have been his highways, trade routes, freight roads, and communications links. Men and women lived with the sea, and every boy dreamed of running away to sea, of commanding a long ocean ship with canvas sails crowded one above the other until the topmost sail, the moonsail, pushed clouds aside. A historian wrote: "Never, in these United States, has the brain of man conceived, or the hand of man fashioned, so perfect a thing as the clipper ship.... The *Flying Cloud* was our Rheims, the *Sovereign of the Seas* our Parthenon, the *Lightning* our Amiens; but they were monuments carved from snow. For a brief moment of time

they flashed their splendor around the world, then disappeared with the sudden completeness of the wild pigeon."

There came a time when the steamship's machinery became more reliable than sail: not as dependent on the strength of the wind, requiring fewer men to tend its boilers than the crew of a wind ship. The steamships produced a loud racket, a satisfying plume of smoke, a churning wake of rust and fuel oil, and profit, much profit. The steamer was modern. It sounded and smelled like progress. The clipper ships that cut their wakes through a million boys' dreams were dismasted. The hulls that carried fragrant teas and spices were filled with bulk cargo, and the quarterdecks that rolled under their young captains—the heroes of their age— were skipperless as the old hulks were towed meekly behind steam tugs, up and down the coast, barging coal, ore, coke, scrap iron, garbage. The age of sail had passed.

Then why am I wearing down my penpoint to tell you about a dead item, something long gone and — perhaps—useless? If I am to make a book with the whole truth, I must answer that question.

ost forms of transportation work against natural forces, using engines and machinery to overcome inertia, friction, and gravity, excluding the influence of the elements as much as possible. Moving in a sailboat depends on your harmony with the forces of nature; you are not overcoming the forces of nature, but moving with them.

o be in harmony with the forces of nature, you must know them intimately. A truthful book may help, but a real acquaintance with sea and moving air is indispensable. Here is where this book may fail at the whole truth: I cannot build spray into page 22, I cannot have the foghorn start its phomphing as you open page 59, I cannot write and draw the funky smell of low tide on page 52. You yourself must find those things and more. No book, at the end of its writing, seems fit and whole. Hemingway's last chapter for *Death In the Afternoon* begins: "If this were enough of a book..." I confess to a similar sadness at the lack of so much in these pages. I am a learner, as we are all learners on the water, and though I know this cannot be all of your sea lesson, I hope it can begin it.

Jan Adams

wareham, massachusetts
new year's day, 1973

9

Theory the gull and the shark

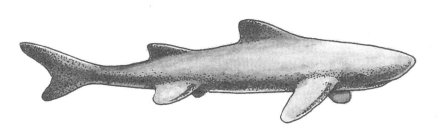

What makes a sailboat go? The wind, you say, the wind blows it along. And so it does, but the wind also blows leaves and milkweed seeds along, throwing them into walls and trees and scraping them along the ground. Good skippers, as you might guess, make at least some attempt to avoid rocks and trees and walls. Then there is something more: a sailboat is moved by the wind in a controlled way that is decided by a simple, subtle law of physics. Once you know how the law operates, you will know how every sailboat works.

Daniel Bernoulli was a Swiss scientist who, in 1738, discovered that the pressure within a moving stream of fluid decreased if the fluid moved faster. (A fluid is a liquid or a gas.) That lessening of pressure in a stream of fluid is now called the *BERNOULLI EFFECT*, and it is easy to see for yourself:

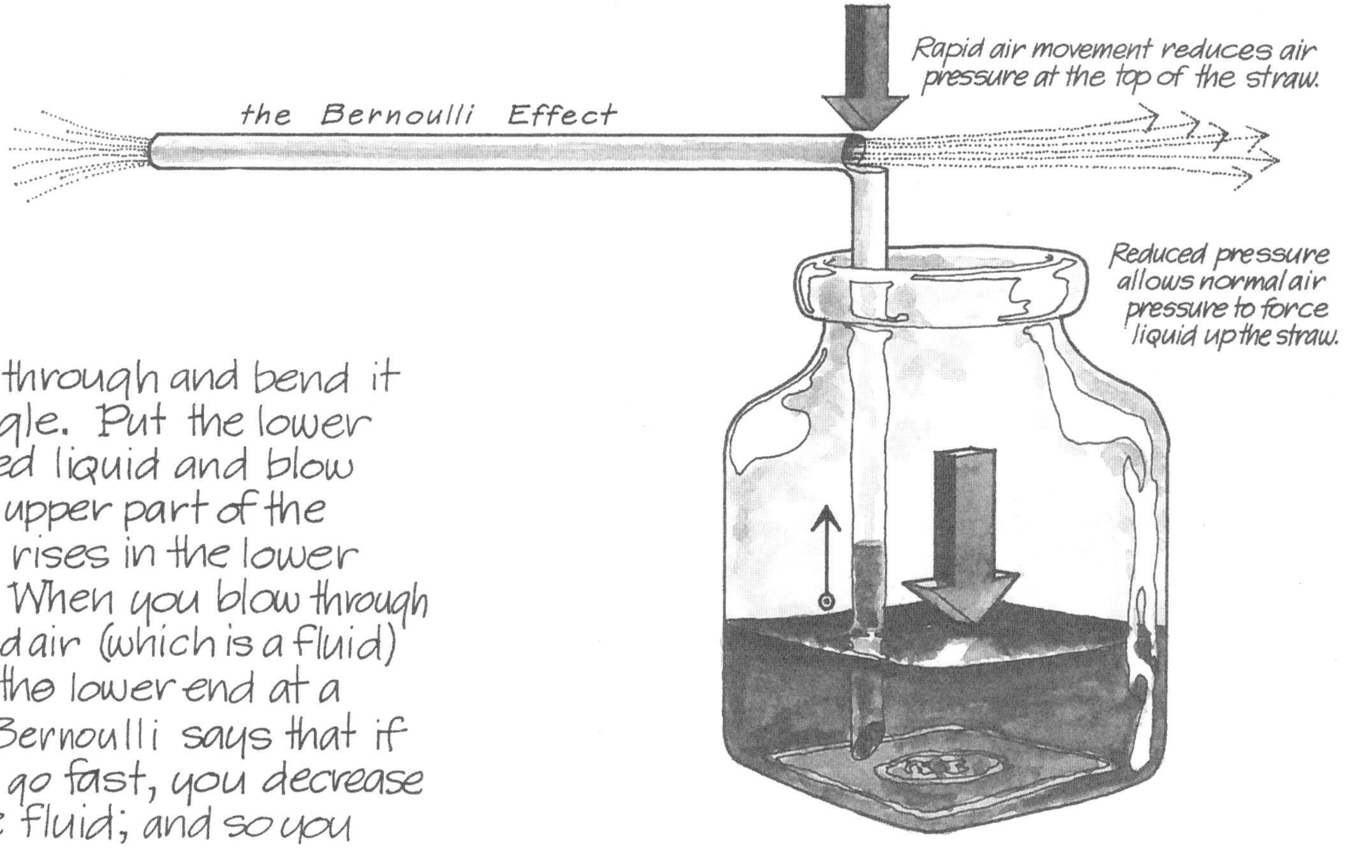

the Bernoulli Effect

Rapid air movement reduces air pressure at the top of the straw.

Reduced pressure allows normal air pressure to force liquid up the straw.

Cut a straw almost through and bend it over at a right angle. Put the lower end in some colored liquid and blow hard through the upper part of the straw — the liquid rises in the lower end of the straw. When you blow through the straw, you send air (which is a fluid) across the top of the lower end at a high speed. Mr. Bernoulli says that if you make a fluid go fast, you decrease the pressure in the fluid; and so you decrease the pressure in the air at the top of the straw. The normal air pressure pushing at the surface of the colored liquid is now greater than the pressure at the top of the straw, and so the normal air pressure pushes the liquid up the straw.

Daniel Bernoulli, straws, and air pressure would have very little to do with sail-boats if it were not for a special shape called the Airfoil.

11

The Airfoil looks like a long teardrop, flattened on one side. Though it is a special shape it is certainly not a rare one, occurring in nature as the shape of gulls' wings, of all birds' wings, the shape of sharks and fish and flying squirrels, of things that glide through fluids. When a fluid passes around an airfoil, its flow is split: the air particles on one side travel a fairly straight path, but the particles travelling around the other side have a longer way to go because of the curve. And to rejoin the flow of air, the curving particles must travel <u>faster</u>. You know that when a fluid travels faster, its pressure decreases, and so the pressure is less on one side of the airfoil.

An airplane uses that pressure difference by having two long airfoils attached to its sides — the wings. As the airplane taxis down the runway, air flows around the airfoils of the wings at greater and greater speeds, until the pressure just above the wings is reduced to the point that air pressure under the wings can lift the plane from the ground. Long before the airplane, though, men were using the airfoil to propel boats.

the airfoil

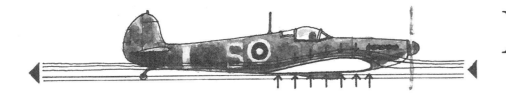

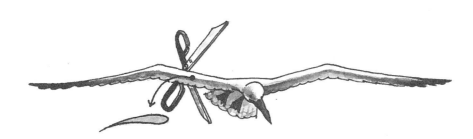

Looking at a sailboat from above, the sail filled with wind forms an airfoil. As the wind passes around that airfoil, pressure on one side is greater than the pressure on the other side. The greater pressure forces the sail in its direction, and the boat can go with the sail. By adjusting the position of the sail in relationship to the hull, the sailor can persuade the wind to take him any watery place he wishes to go.

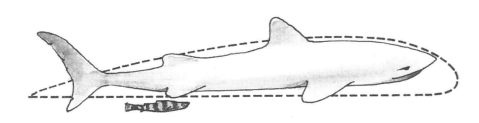

vectors

2 small ants pulling a peanut
ARE THE SAME AS
One large ant pulling the peanut

JUST AS

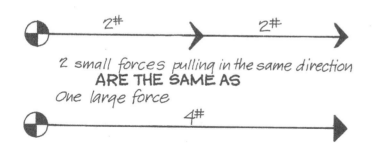

2#   2#

2 small forces pulling in the same direction
ARE THE SAME AS
One large force

4#

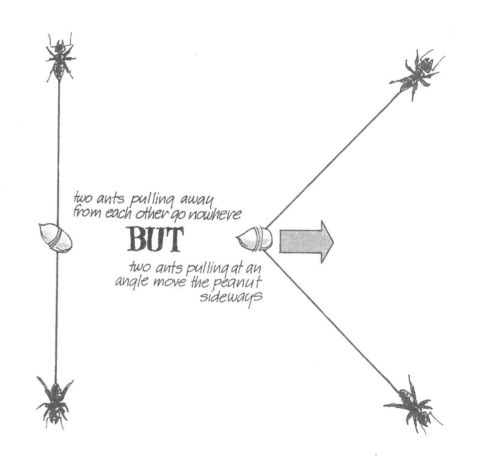

two ants pulling away
from each other go nowhere

BUT

two ants pulling at an
angle move the peanut
sideways

14

A Vector is a force with a direction. If you are holding a 10 pound bag of apple peels, it is only a potential force, but if you throw it in the direction of a passing goose, it is a vector.

That a single directed force – a vector – can be equal to two smaller forces at a right (square) angle to one another (these are called the *Component Forces* of the vector) is extremely important to sailors because of the special way a sailboat uses those component forces.

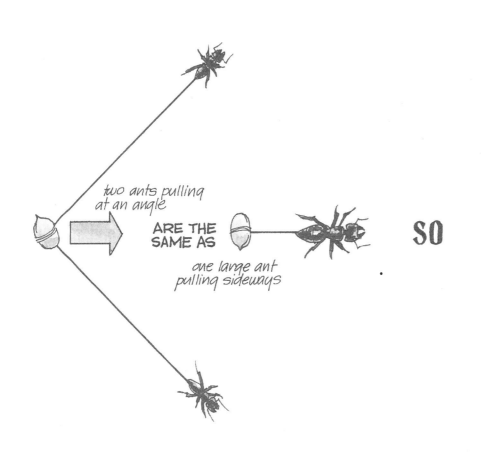

two ants pulling at an angle

ARE THE SAME AS

one large ant pulling sideways

SO

one large ant pulling at an angle

CAN BE THE SAME AS

two smaller ants pulling at a right angle.

JUST AS

One large vector

CAN BE THE SAME AS

two smaller vectors at right angles

10#

8.2#

5.75#

vectors and the sail

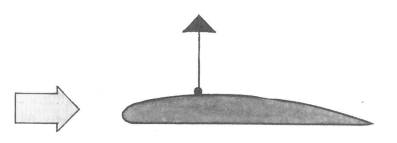

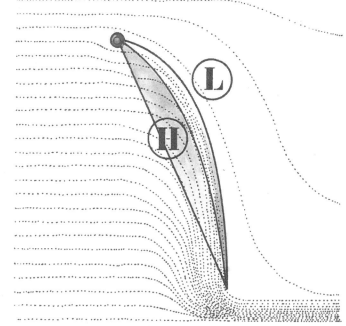

When the wind blows into and across the airfoil of a sail, the pressure on the side toward the wind is high because of the collision of air particles against it, and the pressure on the opposite side is lower because of the airfoil effect of the sail.

Just as the shark's pectoral fins stabilize his smooth glide and prevent his slipping sideways, the sailboat uses a fin to cancel the effect of the vector's sideway component force. Some boats have a movable fin that can be drawn up into the hull, called a <u>centerboard.</u> Some boats have a fin shaped into the hull called the <u>keel</u>. A few boats have twin fins, very like a shark's, called <u>bilge keels</u>.

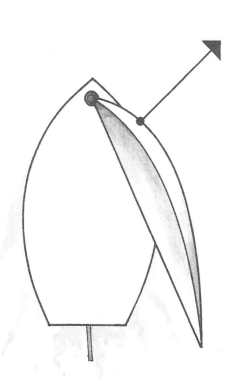

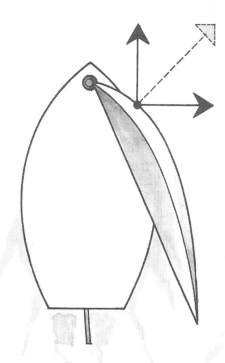

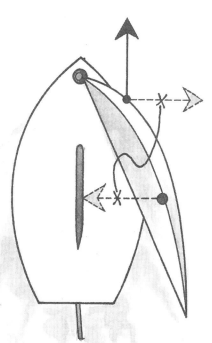

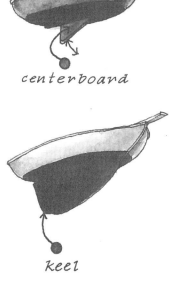

centerboard

keel

bilge keels

Between the high and low pressure areas a vector is created.

That single force can be the same as two component forces: one pulling forward, one pulling sideways.

The side force from the sail is cancelled by the centerboard or keel, leaving only a force pulling forward.

17

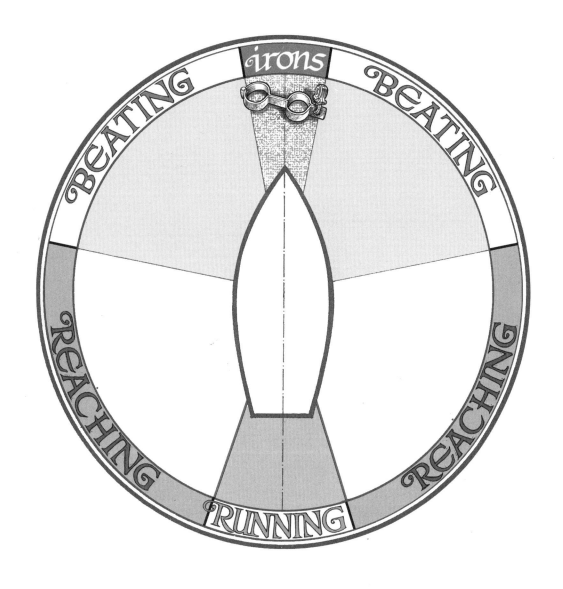

points of sail

A sailcraft's relationship to the wind direction is its "point of sail". When the wind is behind the boat pushing it along, the point of sail is *Running*. The point of sail for a boat with the wind at its side is *Reaching*. With the wind ahead, the boat is *Beating*. These are the basic points of sail, and for each point, the wind drives in a distinct way. For each point of sail there is a set of cautions and conditions that the wind and water demand of a boat. We begin with *Running*

This is a Viking longship built around 810 A.D. in Norway. The wind is behind it; it is *Running*. A long pole (or spar) has been hoisted up the mast and from it strains the simple squaresail, pulling the ship with it. The collision of air particles on the windward side of the sail raises the pressure there. Between the high pressure and the normal pressure on the leeward (pronounced *loo´-ward*, the side away from the wind) a force vector is created and the boat is propelled.

The longship is steered by a paddle-like rudder attached to the rear (or *stern*) of the ship, called a *steering-board*. Most men are right-handed and so it was most convenient when lashed to the right side. The right side of the ship became known as the *steerboard* side, and from shouting across windy decks the word was worn down to "starboard". Now the right hand side of any ship is the starboard side

Open to the weather, offering no shelter except a tent that could be set up on deck, the longships were still strong and seaworthy craft for their brave Viking masters.

wind

19

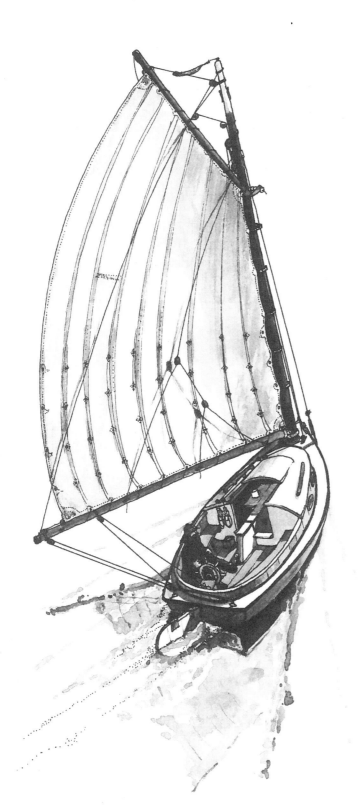

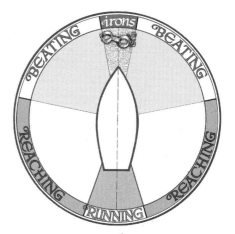

reaching

With the wind at its side, this Cape Cod Catboat is *Reaching*. When *reaching*, the boat is propelled in some part by the air pressure on the windward side, but primarily by the airfoil effect of the sail's shape. When *running* before the wind, the force that drives the sail has no side-way component, but when *reaching*, the center board or keel is important to resist that side-force.

The *boom* (the wooden spar at the bottom of the sail) controls the angle of the sail, and it has been eased out until it is working at its most efficient —

this is called *trimming sail*. If the wind shifts, the skipper will have to *trim sail* again by bringing the boom in or letting it out until the sail is full of wind, but close enough to the direction of the wind to <u>almost</u> flap along the leading edge. When the sail flaps, it *luffs*, and the leading edge of the sail is called the *luff*.

uses its broad base of flotation to resist the tipping — called *heeling* — just as a wide base makes a lamp less likely to tip over. Deep boats can be slimmer because the heavy weight at the bottom of their keel resists *heeling*.

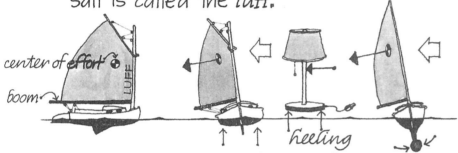

center of effort
LUFF
boom
heeling

weather helm

Every square foot of sail, if it is a well-made sail and if the skipper *trims* it properly, contributes some force to the effort of moving the boat. If all the forces and their directions were added up, a sail's power would seem to come from a single spot that boat designers call the *center of effort*. The *center of effort* is high above the hull, and when the wind is at the boat's side (as it is when *reaching*), that high force tries to tip the boat on its side. A shallow boat like the Catboat is wide, and

If we nailed a long plank across the boat and if we all pushed on the outboard end of the plank, we would turn the boat around. When the boom is eased out for *reaching* or *running*, the *center of effort* lies outboard and the force of the sail tries to turn the boat into the wind. This turning tendency is called *weather helm* (because *helming* is steering, and the wind's direction is the direction weather comes from). When *heeled* the situation is complicated, since one side of the hull drags in the water more than the other.

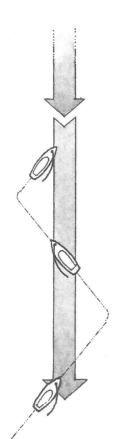

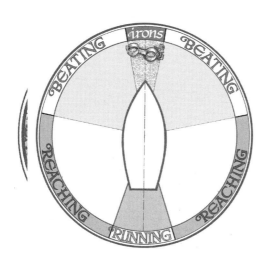

beating

No sailboat can sail directly into the wind, but the airfoil shape of the sail can produce a vector that propels it at an angle toward the wind, so it can move in the wind's general direction. When a sailcraft is moving toward the wind, it is _beating_. By sailing at an angle to the left of the wind's direction, and then at an angle to the right, a sailboat can make a zig-zag course anywhere to windward. These two Tempests are _beating_, or moving into the wind—one sailing at its closest angle to the right of the wind, the other sailing to the left of the wind.

wind

Running **Reaching** **Beating**
←∘ ∘—→ ∘———→
little leeway *greatest leeway*

When the vectors that propel a sailboat _running_, _reaching_, and _beating_, are resolved, as they are above, you can see that the greatest side-force occurs as the boat is _beating_. When _beating_, then, the centerboard or keel is most necessary to prevent _leeway_ (moving sideways, away from the wind), and the boat is _heeled_ at an angle that decreases the efficiency of sails and hull. To regain that efficiency, the crews of these Tempests are _hiking_ (leaning out over the windward edge of the boat to tip the boat up).

If the boat is steered straight into the wind, the sails will only _luff_ (flap). They will not be full of wind and will stop working. The boat will stop with them. Since no water will be flowing around the _rudder_, it will no longer steer. In this helpless condition, the boat is _in irons_.

23

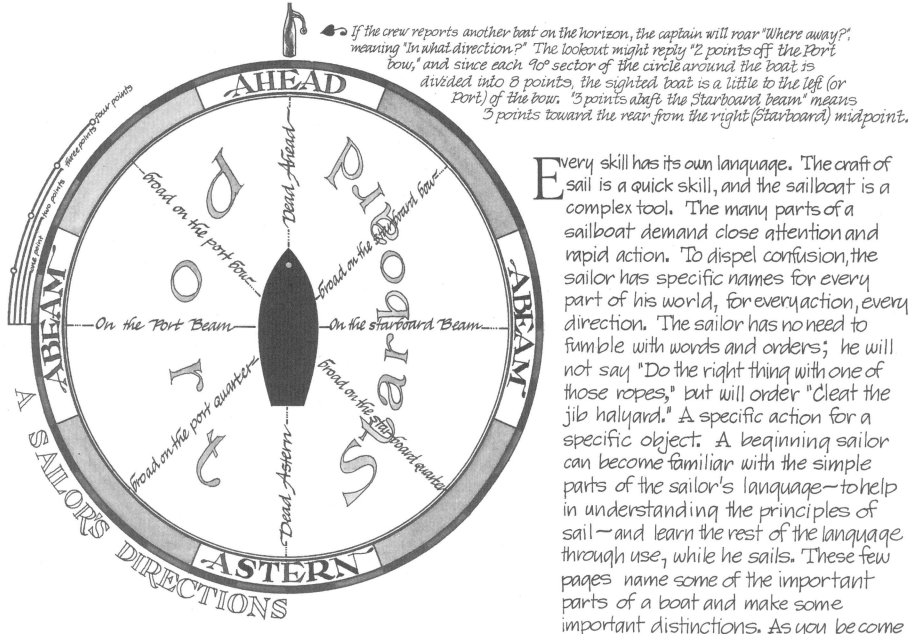

If the crew reports another boat on the horizon, the captain will roar "Where away?", meaning "In what direction?" The lookout might reply "2 points off the Port bow," and since each 90° sector of the circle around the boat is divided into 8 points, the sighted boat is a little to the left (or Port) of the bow. "3 points abaft the Starboard beam" means 3 points toward the rear from the right (Starboard) midpoint.

AHEAD

Dead Ahead

Port — Starboard

Broad on the port bow — Broad on the starboard bow

On the Port Beam — On the starboard Beam

Broad on the port quarter — Broad on the starboard quarter

Dead Astern

ABEAM — **ABEAM**

ASTERN

one point · two points · three points · four points

A SAILOR'S DIRECTIONS

A Sailor's Language

Every skill has its own language. The craft of sail is a quick skill, and the sailboat is a complex tool. The many parts of a sailboat demand close attention and rapid action. To dispel confusion, the sailor has specific names for every part of his world, for every action, every direction. The sailor has no need to fumble with words and orders; he will not say "Do the right thing with one of those ropes," but will order "Cleat the jib halyard." A specific action for a specific object. A beginning sailor can become familiar with the simple parts of the sailor's language—to help in understanding the principles of sail—and learn the rest of the language through use, while he sails. These few pages name some of the important parts of a boat and make some important distinctions. As you become more experienced, you will become more pleased at the concise practicality of the sailor's language as a way for a sailor to talk to another sailor.

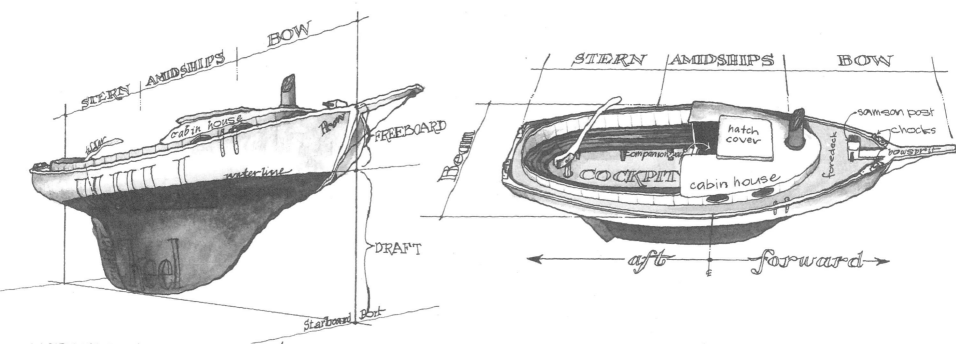

AMIDSHIPS~ the middle part of a vessel/ BEAM~ a direction: across the boat, at right angles to its length/ BOW~ the forward part of a vessel/ BOWSPRIT~ a spar projecting from the bow of a vessel/ CABIN-HOUSE~ a structure on deck enclosing the cabin quarters below/ CENTERBOARD TRUNK~ a box built into the hull of a boat to contain the centerboard when raised/ COCKPIT~ a depression or well in the deck (usually aft) from which the boat is steered/ COMPANIONWAY~ passageway from deck to the cabin below/ DRAFT~ the depth a vessel requires to float/ FOREDECK~ the foremost part of the deck, forward of the cabin house/ FREEBOARD~ height of the hull above the waterline/ KEEL~ the main member of a vessel's construction, lying along the lowest ridge of the hull; ALSO, a deep, fixed fin counteracting sideslip/ PROW~ the rising point of the bow/ RUDDER~ the movable fin that steers a vessel/ STERN~ the rear part of a ship/ STERN-SHEETS~ a seat across the stern of a rowing or sailing vessel/ THWART~ a seat across a rowing or sailing vessel/ TILLER~ a length of wood or metal controlling the rudder/ TRANSOM~ a plate forming the hull's stern-piece/ WATERLINE~ the level at which a hull floats in the water

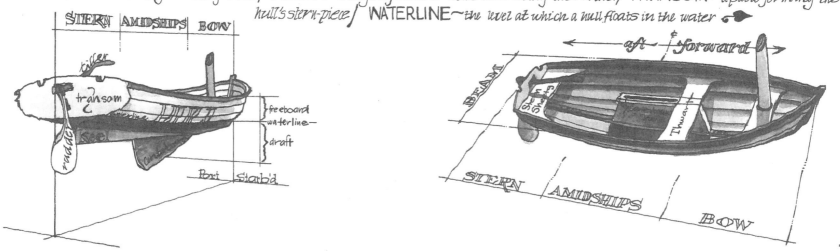

25

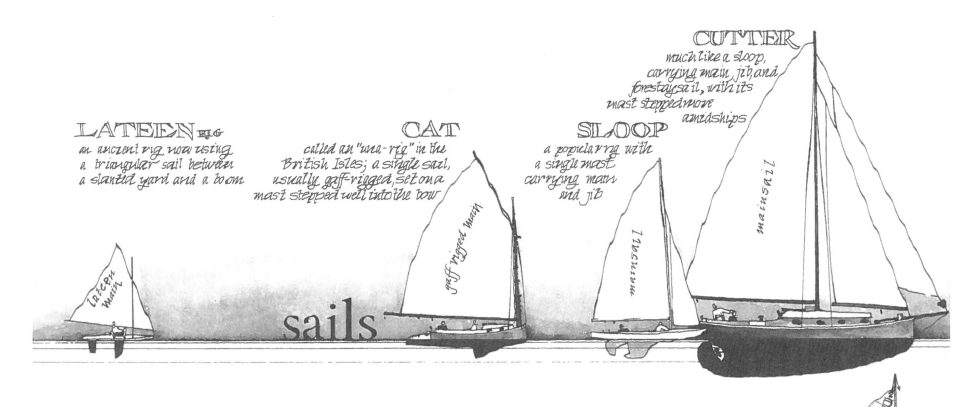

LATEEN rig
an ancient rig now using
a triangular sail between
a slanted yard and a boom

lateen main

CAT
called an "una-rig" in the
British Isles; a single sail,
usually gaff-rigged, set on a
mast stepped well into the bow

gaff rigged main

SLOOP
a popular rig with
a single mast
carrying main
and jib

mainsail

CUTTER
much like a sloop,
carrying main, jib, and
forestaysail, with its
mast stepped more
amidships

mainsail

sails

Sails are the driving heart of a sailcraft, and
a great part of the excitement of travelling by
the wind: a sailor has a bright expanse of
sewn cloth quivering above him like a flag
in the wind. Most types of sailcraft carry
more than a single sail. During the great
age of sail there were dozens of sail
configurations, but today there are only
a few predominant types: the _gaff-headed_
sail or the _marconi-rigged_ — sometimes
called _jib-headed_ — sail is used as a main
and mizzen rig. The _headsails_ (_jibs_ and

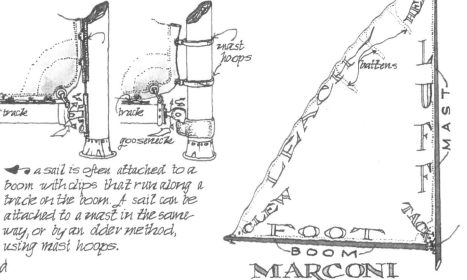

mast hoops

track *track*

gooseneck

➤ a sail is often attached to a
boom with clips that run along a
track on the boom. A sail can be
attached to a mast in the same
way, or by an older method,
using mast hoops.

HEAD
battens
LEACH
LUFF
MAST
CLEW
FOOT
TACK
BOOM

MARCONI

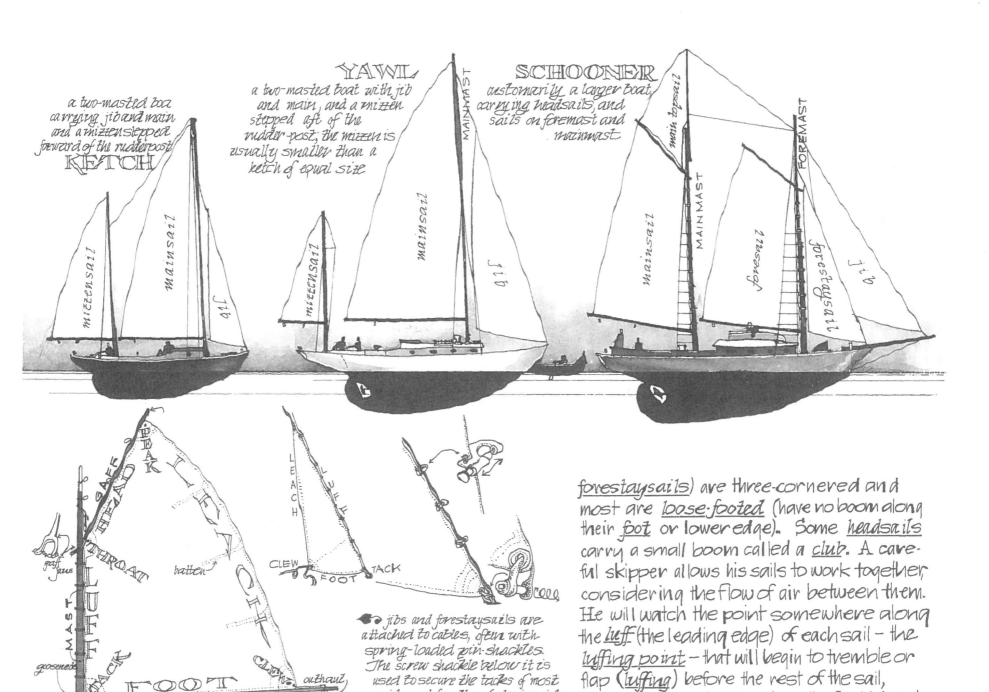

KETCH
a two-masted boat carrying jib and main and a mizzen stepped forward of the rudderpost

YAWL
a two-masted boat with jib and main, and a mizzen stepped aft of the rudder-post; the mizzen is usually smaller than a ketch of equal size

SCHOONER
customarily a larger boat, carrying headsails, and sails on foremast and mainmast

mizzensail · *mainsail* · *jib*

mizzensail · *mainsail* · *jib*

mainsail · MAINMAST · *foresail* · FOREMAST · *forestaysail* · *jib*

GAFF · HEAD · PEAK
LEACH
MAST · LUFF · THROAT
gaff jaws
batten
HULL
TACK
gooseneck
LEACH · CLEW
FOOT · BOOM · GAFF
outhaul

LEACH · LUFF
CLEW · TACK
FOOT

jibs and forestaysails are attached to cables, often with spring-loaded pin-shackles. The screw shackle below it is used to secure the tacks of most sails, and for other fastening jobs.

forestaysails) are three-cornered and most are loose-footed (have no boom along their foot or lower edge). Some headsails carry a small boom called a club. A careful skipper allows his sails to work together, considering the flow of air between them. He will watch the point somewhere along the luff (the leading edge) of each sail – the luffing point – that will begin to tremble or flap (luffing) before the rest of the sail, telling him when to trim his sails for highest efficiency.

rigging

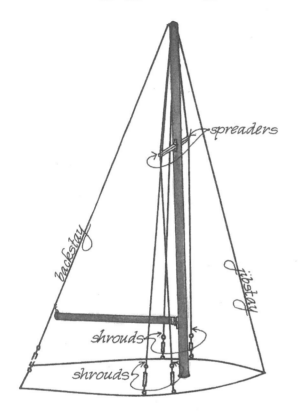

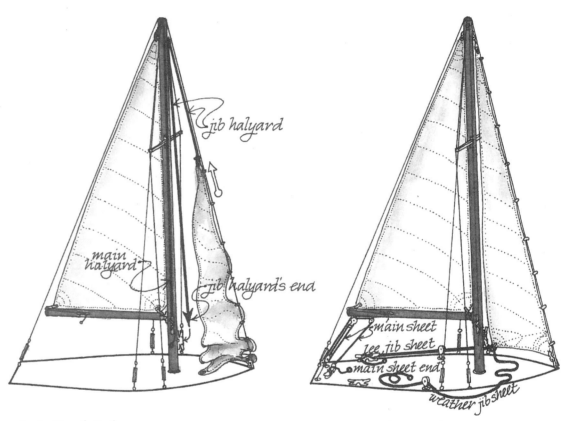

SHROUDS/STAYS

shrouds and stays support masts: stays support in a fore and aft direction, and shrouds support ATHWARTSHIPS (from side to side). Because they are not moved in use, they are called STANDING RIGGING. On contemporary sailcraft, standing rigging is usually stainless steel cable ☙➤

HALYARDS

halyards hoist sails. Here, the jib halyard is shackled to the head of the jib and hauled through a block (a pulley) at the mast-head. The halyards run down alongside the mast or even inside a hollow mast. When the sail is taut at its height, the halyard is made fast to a cleat at the base of the mast ☙➤

SHEETS

sheets control the angle of sails to the wind. A sail with a boom normally requires only one sheet, while a loose-footed headsail is usually controlled by a sheet on each side of the vessel, running aft to cleats on either side of the cockpit ☙➤

28

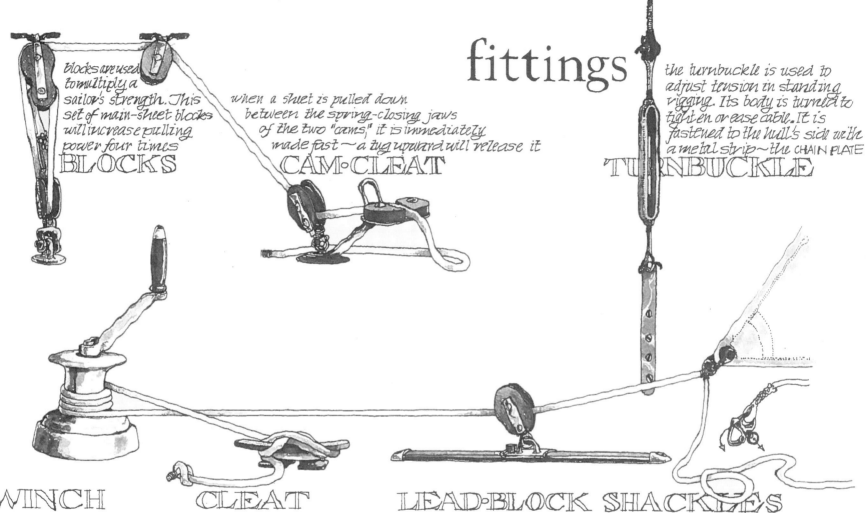

fittings

BLOCKS

blocks are used to multiply a sailor's strength. This set of main-sheet blocks will increase pulling power four times

CAM·CLEAT

when a sheet is pulled down between the spring-closing jaws of the two "cams," it is immediately made fast ~ a tug upward will release it

TURNBUCKLE

the turnbuckle is used to adjust tension in standing rigging. Its body is turned to tighten or ease cable. It is fastened to the hull's side with a metal strip~ the CHAIN PLATE

WINCH

the winch is another method of multiplying strength, often used to manage the sheets of large jibs. Several turns of the sheet are taken around the drum ~ bottom to top, and clockwise ~ the sheet is hauled in, first by hand, then cranked in

CLEAT

cleats are used almost everywhere a line must be made fast.

LEAD·BLOCK

the lead-block is used to bring the jibsheet from the jib's clew at the correct angle. This one slides on a track to accommodate different jib sizes.

SHACKLES

this jib is made fast to the jibsheets with a screw shackle through a grommet in its clew. Spring-loaded snap-shackles also connect sails to halyards and sheets

29

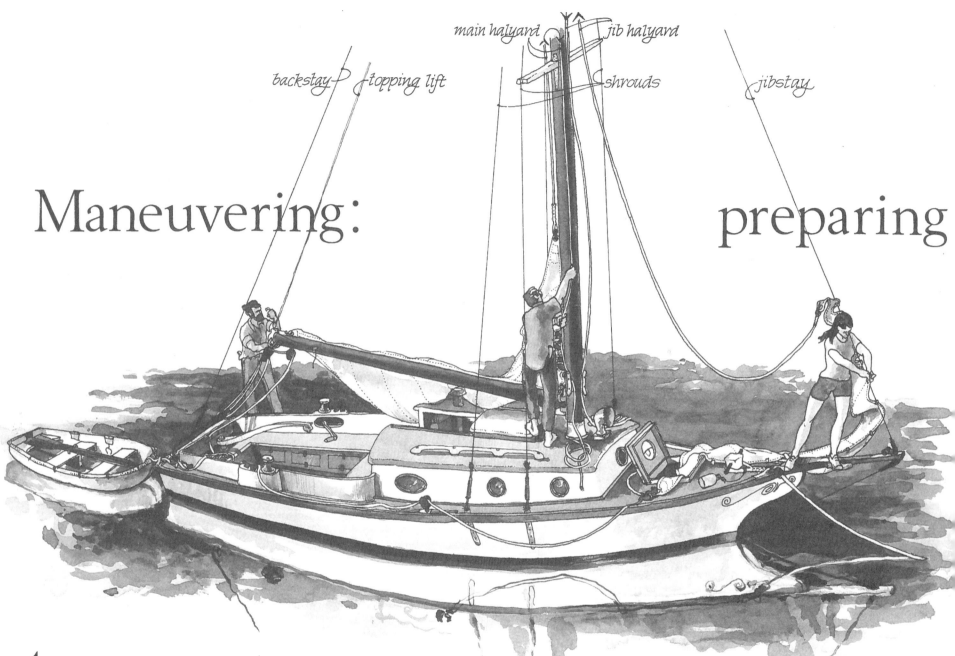

Maneuvering: preparing

backstay   topping lift   main halyard   jib halyard   shrouds   jibstay

This sloop's crew is preparing to get under way (getting ready to go). the skipper has eased (let out) the mainsheet, and is now easing the <u>Topping Lift</u> (the line that holds up the boom when the sail is not supporting it. the dinghy has been drawn up close to the stern for maneuvering, but will be towed further astern outside the anchorage. the crew member on the cabin house is about to raise the mainsail while the crew on the bowsprit is <u>Bending</u> (attaching) the jib to the jibstay. a boat <u>Makes Sail</u> from stern to bow, so that headsails will not push the bow away from the wind without the drag of sails astern 🐟▶

to get under way

3 "Sheet the jib" as the boat swings with the wind on its side, the sails fill and begin to pull. the jib is sheeted in on the lee side, and the boat <u>Makes Way</u> (moves forward). this vessel is off on her journey 🙢

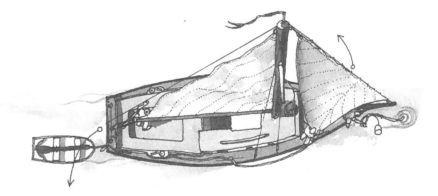

2 "back the jib" another crew member holds the jib out to starboard so the backwinded jib will push the bow around to port. the skipper reverses his tiller so the stern will swing to starboard as the boat backs up. 🙢

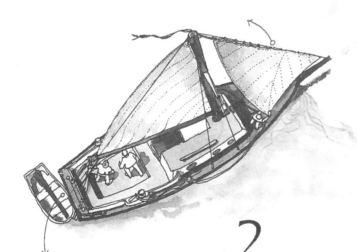

1 "drop the mooring" one crew member uncleats the mooring pendant and the boat is free; it begins to drift back away from the wind with its sails luffing, in irons 🙢

31

This ketch (a *Rozinante* designed by Mr. L. Francis Herreshoff) is maneuvering into the wind. While making its zig-zag course, it has the wind on one side, then the other: with the wind coming over the starboard bow, the boat is on its _starboard tack_; with the wind on the port bow, the boat is on its _port tack_. Changing from one tack to the other, the boat is _tacking_ or _coming about_. A series of tacks will bring this vessel up into the wind like the rungs of a ladder.

tacking/coming·about

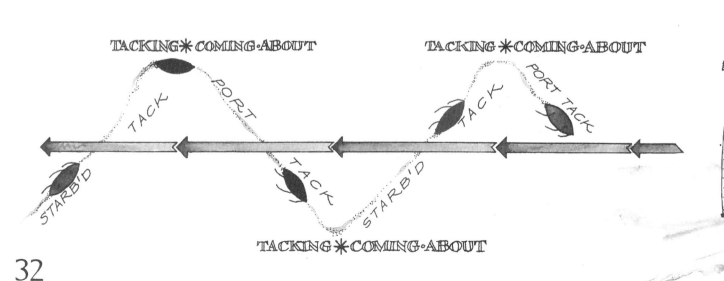

TACKING ✳ COMING·ABOUT

PORT TACK

TACK

STARB'D

TACKING ✳ COMING·ABOUT

PORT TACK

TACK

STARB'D

TACKING ✳ COMING·ABOUT

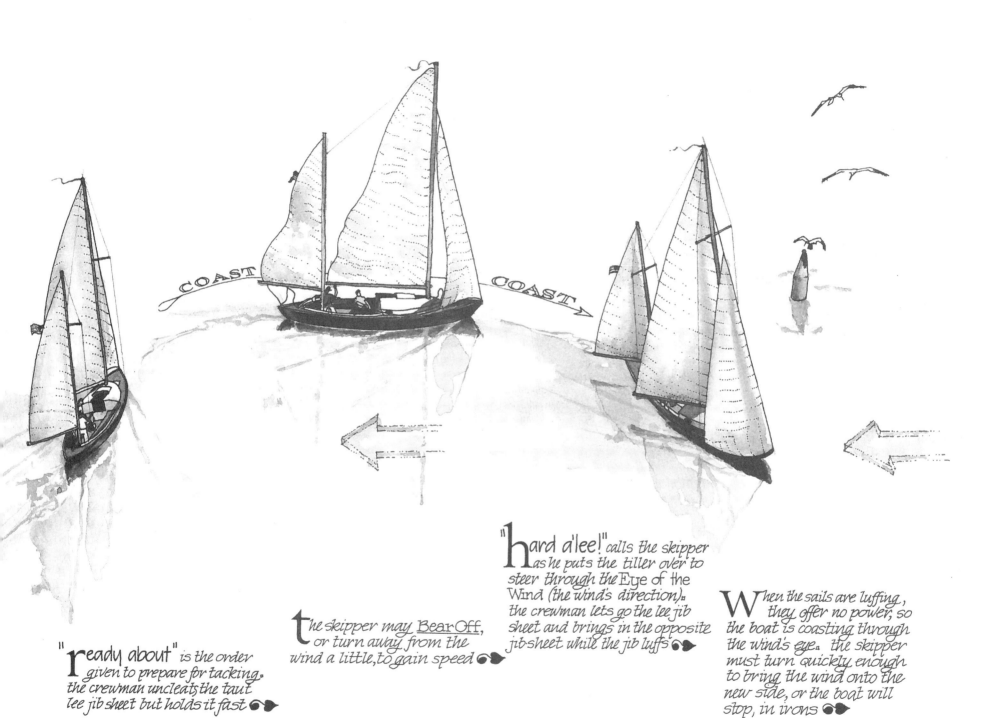

COAST

COAST

"**r**eady about" is the order given to prepare for tacking. the crewman uncleats the taut lee jib sheet but holds it fast 👁️▶

the skipper may Bear Off, or turn away from the wind a little, to gain speed 👁️▶

"**h**ard a'lee!" calls the skipper as he puts the tiller over to steer through the Eye of the Wind (the wind's direction). the crewman lets go the lee jib sheet and brings in the opposite jib sheet while the jib luffs 👁️▶

When the sails are luffing, they offer no power, so the boat is coasting through the wind's eye. the skipper must turn quickly enough to bring the wind onto the new side, or the boat will stop, in irons 👁️▶

33

Bringing the wind from one side of the sail to the other by steering the stern through the eye of the wind is _gybing_, a maneuver for changing direction when running.

Running before the wind is the most difficult point of sail for a small boat, and the most dangerous, because of the possibility of an accidental _gybe_. *pronounced & sometimes spelled "jibe"*

gybing

In tacking, the wind gradually shifts the sail from one side to the other; but in gybing, the wind comes completely around behind the sail before it is thrown across the boat. even in a moderate wind the boom can snap around with enough force to damage the boat and the crew ●●➤

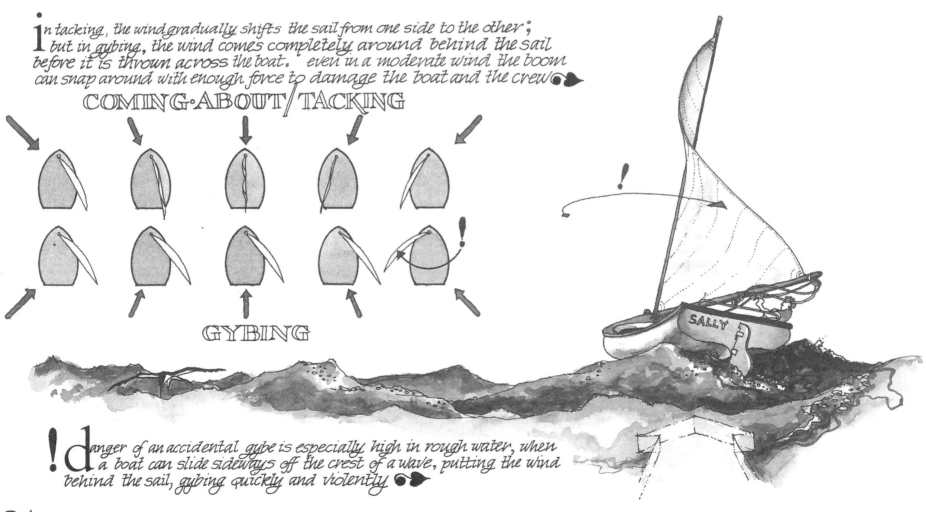

COMING·ABOUT/TACKING

GYBING

SALLY

!d anger of an accidental _gybe_ is especially high in rough water, when a boat can slide sideways off the crest of a wave, putting the wind behind the sail, gybing quickly and violently ●●➤

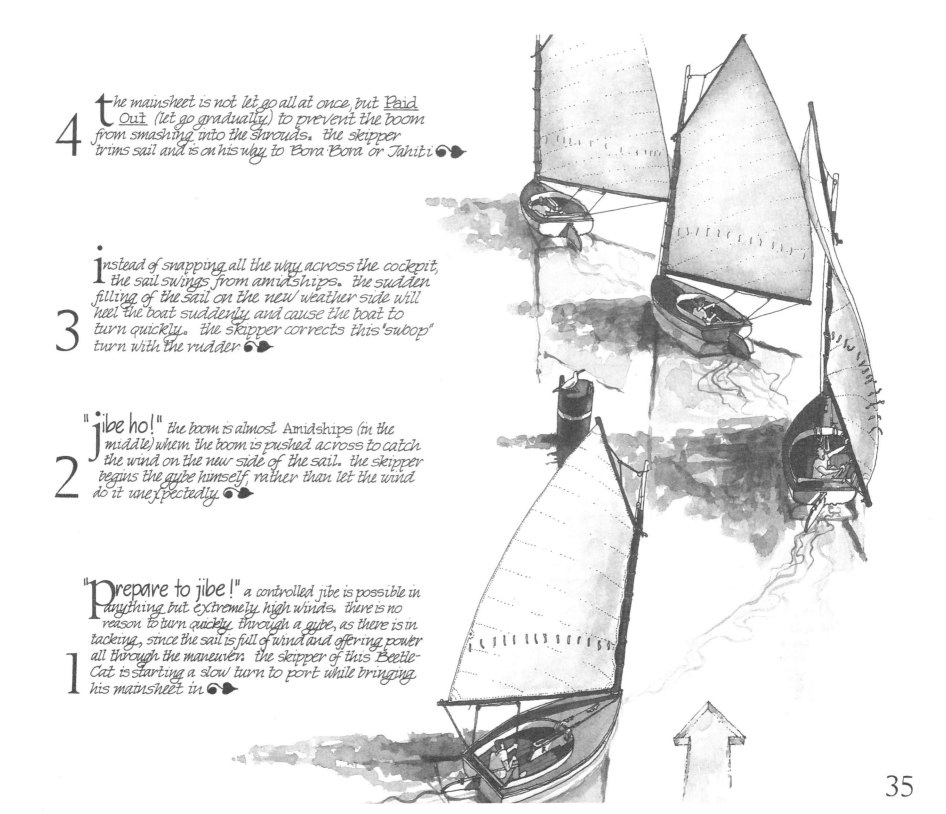

4 the mainsheet is not let go all at once, but <u>Paid Out</u> (let go gradually) to prevent the boom from smashing into the shrouds. the skipper trims sail and is on his way to Bora Bora or Tahiti ❧

3 instead of snapping all the way across the cockpit, the sail swings from amidships. the sudden filling of the sail on the new weather side will heel the boat suddenly and cause the boat to turn quickly. the skipper corrects this "swoop" turn with the rudder ❧

2 "jibe ho!" the boom is almost Amidships (in the middle) when the boom is pushed across to catch the wind on the new side of the sail. the skipper begins the gybe himself, rather than let the wind do it unexpectedly ❧

1 "Prepare to jibe!" a controlled jibe is possible in anything but extremely high winds. there is no reason to turn quickly through a gybe, as there is in tacking, since the sail is full of wind and offering power all through the maneuver. the skipper of this Beetle-Cat is starting a slow turn to port while bringing his mainsheet in ❧

There are ways of boat-handling that faded after the age of working sailboat. _Heaving-to_ was a maneuver repeated many times during a coasting sailor's day.: It is a way of controlling a boat in a stationary position for fishing, pulling lobster pots, or having lunch. It is also a way to ride out a storm, but in heavy weather the sails are shortened (reefed, page 60) or small stormsails are used.

heaving·to

this Stone Horse sloop is <u>hove-to</u> : its main is sheeted in closely, its tiller is lashed to port, and one of its headsails (here, the forestaysail) is <u>backed</u> (sheeted on the weather side). the backed headsail is trying to force the bow to port, but it is overpowered by the larger mainsail, which drives to forward and to star-board under the influence of the tiller. when bow comes up into the wind, the main luffs and loses power, the backed head-sail takes over and forces the bow back to port, the main-sail fills and the cycle begins again.

lashed tiller   backed headsail
close main

Man-Overboard drill should be practiced over and over in every wind, on every point of sail, until the easy retrieval of fallen crew members, blown hats, dropped jackets, and other flotsam, becomes a natural reflex.

man·overboard

"Stand by to gybe!"

something bouyant and easily thrown is always kept in the cockpit, and a length of line for heaving is also handy ●❧

as soon as anything goes overboard, the lifebuoy is thrown near it, and one crew member does nothing but watch the spot ●❧

the boat is quickly jibed and brought around to approach on a reach or a close reach ●❧

the boat is steered for a pickup on the windward bow~ if a crewman is in the water, a line is thrown to haul him in ●❧

RUNNING   BEATING   REACHING

A *mooring* is a permanent anchor; the boat's home. Most moorings are a heavy weight or anchor embedded in the bottom, attached to heavy chain, to lighter chain, to a rope *mooring-pendant* (pronounced "pennant"), and finally to a light line with a buoy. A skipper approaches his mooring from downwind, headsails taken in to keep the bow into the wind. He steers directly to windward, sail luffing, and *shoots* (coasts) to the buoy, losing speed. He tries to gauge the length of his *shoot* so that he stops with his bow beside the buoy. He takes care to *shoot* the buoy at a slight angle, so that he knows on which side he will fall away from the wind if the pendant is fumbled and dropped.

A crew member is waiting in the bow with a boat-hook to catch the line <u>under</u> the buoy (not the loop at the top). The line and buoy are quickly brought aboard, and the heavier *mooring-pendant* with it. Immediately, a quick turn of the pendant is taken around a heavy cleat or the *samson post* (a strong, upright post in the foredeck for line-handling) to absorb the pull of the boat drifting back from the mooring. The pendant is fitted through a chock, the *eye-splice* (a permanent loop) at its end is slipped over the cleat or post, and the buoy line is made fast over the pendant to keep it in place. The boat is home.

mooring

wind

COASTING

wind

docking:

A boat is no creature of the land; its element is deep, open water. The crew of a boat, though, is supplied and provisioned by the land, so contact between the boat and the shore is inevitable. Bringing the fragile hull of a boat up to an unyielding dock can be a delicate maneuver, never executed without forethought and planning.

three winds

Before approaching a dock, _fenders_ of rope, rubber or stuffed canvas are hung on the shore side to prevent the hull from grating against the dock. Ideally, the boat stops dead in the water a foot from the dock, the crewmen step to the dock and make their vessel fast with docking lines. Since a boat has no brakes, it must be stopped by bringing its bow into the wind, sails luffing, or by letting the sails luff to the side, or by lowering the sails. In any case, proper docking is a matter of the skipper's judgment as to how far his boat will _shoot_ (coast) without power.

With the wind ACROSS the face of the dock, this FRIENDSHIP SLOOP (left & below) approaches on a close reach, fenders out and docklines ready, luffing up into the wind parallel to the dock

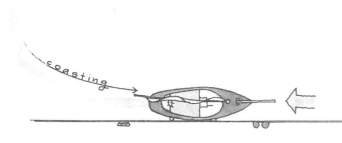

With a wind coming OFF the dock, she approaches beating, turning parallel to the dock while letting her sail luff to the side, her crew must make her fast quickly, before she is blown away from the dock

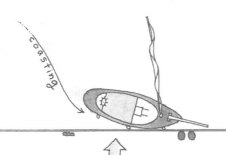

When the wind is blowing ONTO the dock, she approaches on a reach, and lowers her sails some distance away, she coasts to a stop off the face of the dock and allows the wind to drift her in. a larger boat—or any boat in heavy weather—would drop an anchor offshore and back slowly in on the anchor line

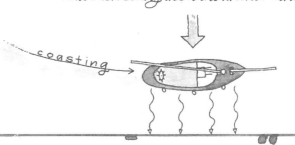

A Sailor's Skills: sea clothes

As cleverly conceived and strongly built as a boat may be, it is helpless alone. The will of a boat, its eyes and thoughts and nerves, are in its crew. To see for a boat, to think and feel for it, and to tend its needs, the crew must have a set of old skills: handiness with lines, an eye for weather and channel buoys, the feel for a dinghy, intimate knowledge of the thousand little things aboard that can go right, or go wrong. The way of a boat, then, is by favor of the wind and by grace of a sailor's skills.

In the old canvas days it was said that a sailor had "one hand for the boat and one for himself," meaning that, aloft in the rigging or on deck, half of his duty was to keep himself safe. A sailor today has even more of an obligation to see to his own safety—and to his comfort, too, if he is to give good service to the boat. He is obliged to keep himself dry and warm, to protect himself from glare, burn and chafe, and to keep from being the object of a man-overboard drill. Choosing proper seafaring clothes is a sailorly skill.

this sailor from the old days of sail has little special clothing. he climbs the rigging best barefoot, his pant legs are cut short to keep them out of the way. he wears a rigging knife on his hip, his hair is plaited into one pigtail, and was sometimes slicked back with tar to keep it out of his eyes ❦

a modern yachtsman may be comfortable at the middle of the season in shorts and a short-sleeved jersey. he wears deck shoes with special non-slip soles to protect himself—and the deck. he has a sailing knife on a lanyard in his pocket, and wears a hat with a brim to protect his eyes from glare

in a rough sea, even strong swimmers should wear life jackets. this sailor is also wearing a life-line around his waist, the other end is made fast to the boat. (a life-line is always advisable when sailing alone) he wears a turtleneck and knit watch-cap against the chill. he has a knife and marlinspike in a sheath

rain or heavy spray brings the foul-weather gear out of the locker. this helmswoman's rubber seaboots could be easily kicked off if she were dunked. her sou'wester rain hat keeps her head dry. Her slicker and rain-pants are bright yellow for high visibility

One of the main distinctions between a sailor and a landsman is the sailor's skill with line. The sailor's world is held and manipulated by lines: the shrouds and stays support the mast, the halyards and sheets raise and control the sails, the mooring pendants, anchor warps and docking lines secure the boat at rest, and hundreds of yards of smaller line lash and stow and tighten and mend all about a vessel 🕶 Line (sailor-men almost never use the word "rope") is made from only about five kinds of fibres, each with qualities that recommend them for different purposes ⇨ Good quality Manila is strong, smooth and durable, but not very elastic. Because sheets and halyards must be set tight without stretch, manilla has been widely used for running rigging. ⇨ Stronger than manila, Dacron line is gentle to the hands and has little enough elasticity to be a more modern choice for sheets and halyards. It has the additional advantage of being a synthetic fibre, impervious to the rot that attacks natural fibres. ⇨ Nylon is wonderfully strong, rotproof, and very elastic. It is ideal for docking lines and anchor lines (called anchor *warps*) because its stretching acts as a cushioning spring against the surge of the waves. Yacht braid is nylon line with an outer shell and an inner core. Its elasticity is re-duced, and this easily handled line is sometimes used as sheets and even halyards. ⇨ Hemp is a fairly strong

natural fibre that stretches very little. It lacks the natural oils, however, that retard decay, and so does not stand up well to weathering. The old sailors soaked it with tar to prevent rot, and used it as standing rigging. Hemp is most common now as Marline, tar-soaked cord of two strands used for hundreds of jobs aboardship. ⇨ Cotton is not a strong fibre, but it is soft and pliable and white. Kind to the hands, it is used for flag halyards, fancy lashings, decorative work and other light duty work. 🕶 Marline, single-braid nylon and dacron, and all line, twine and cord under about ¼", is called *Small Stuff*. Small stuff is indispensible aboardship. Synthetic braids are used to lash (tie down) anchors, to secure canvas sailcovers and hatchcovers, to lash objects below against rolling, and for tough utility jobs all over a boat. Marline's (pronounced mar'-linn) tarry consistency binds against itself and makes its knots hold particularly well. That, plus its strength and hemp's low elasticity, make marline a choice for *siezings*, permanent knots that hold lines tightly together. Waxed linen and polyester twines are used for *whipping*, closely wrapping the ends of ropes to prevent strands from unwrapping or braid from fraying. No working length of *laid* (stranded) or braided rope should be without a whipping 🕶

Line

making fast

Halyards and mooring lines are cleated and secured with a HALF-HITCH (the last two parts of the cleating sequence below). Because a small boat's sheets must sometimes be CAST-OFF (released) quickly, they are seldom half-hitched. Rather, the turns around the horns are secured with a couple of turns around the base of the cleat.

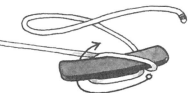

Cleats are the principal holdfasts. The main sheet cleat and a dozen brothers keep a sailboat in working tension, and the sequence of cleating a line should become a smooth instinct.

the line is taken around the base of the cleat under _both_ horns before it crosses over.

the line crisscrosses the top once (twice if the load is great) passing under the horns.

a loop is thrown around the fingers so the end of the line is under the last crossing.

the loop is slipped over the horn and snugged ~ the pressure of the last crossing holds it firm.

TAKE A TURN is the first rule of making fast a line that will carry strain. Forces that would pluck a sailor off the deck can be comfortably held if the line is wrapped around a well-fastened post or cleat.

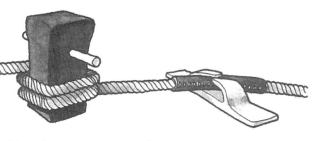

LEAD FAIR is another important rule. Anchor, mooring and docking lines should be lead overside through a chock that minimizes chafe as the boat shifts and rocks. (Mooring lines often have chafe gaurds at the cleat section.)

Most of the strain is taken by a turn around the post ~ two or three if the load is great.

The line is taken around the Norman Pin on both sides.

A loop is made so the end of the line is under the last crossing.

The loop is slipped around the pin and snugged. The pressure of the crossing holds it firm.

The Samson Post is a beam reaching into the structure of a boat. It is a secure device used to make the mooring pendant and anchor warp fast. There is often a metal pin, called a Norman Pin, fitted through the post as an aid to cleating.

It is as important to know how and where to use knots as to know how to tie them, and it is as important as tying them to *fair up* (shape them with your fingers) before load is applied. # Knots

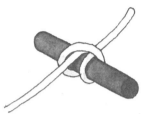

the **CLOVE HITCH** *is a simple knot applied to posts and bollards, non-slippery round surfaces, to with-stand right-angle pull.*

the line is taken once around

the line is passed across the original lead and around

it is tucked under the crossing

fair up by moving both turns together and snugging both leads.

the **ROLLING HITCH** *is for pull lengthwise along a line or spar.*

two turns are taken back toward the direction of the pull

the line is passed across the turns and around again

it is tucked under the crossing

the turns are moved together and both leads are snugged

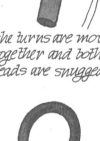

the **ANCHOR HITCH** *attaches a line to a ring or small diameter object.*

the line is taken through twice

it is passed across the lead and tucked through both turns

after snugging, the line is taken around and tucked again

the hitch is snugged and faired up by working it with fingers.

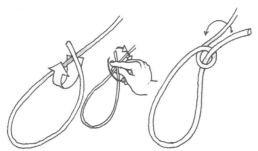 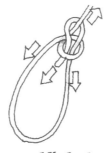 

the end is laid over the lead, both are turned under and toward you...

leaving the end through the loop formed. the end is passed around

around the lead and down through the loop, all lines are snugged

the knot is released by pushing forward the loop around the original lead.

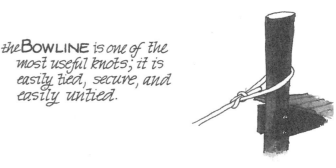

the **BOWLINE** is one of the most useful knots; it is easily tied, secure, and easily untied.

◄ **hitch** MAKING A LINE FAST TO AN OBJECT

▲ **noose** A SECURE LOOP

▼ **bend** MAKING ONE LINE FAST TO ANOTHER LINE

SHEET BEND

the sheet bend is formed like the bowline / one end is laid over the other / together they are turned under and toward you to form a loop with the lower end inside it / the lower end is passed around the upper line and tucked back through the loop / all lines are snugged.

This is one of the most secure bends, a heavy duty knot.

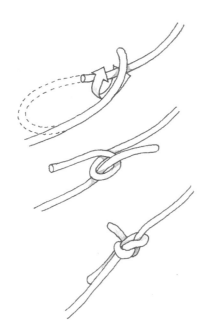

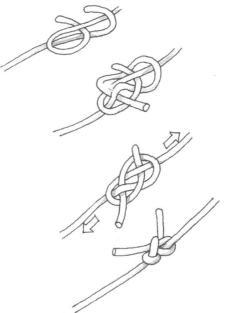

CARRICK BEND

a loop is made of the upper line with its end under the lead / the lower line is placed under the loop and over the upper line / the lower end is taken under the upper end and under its own lead which is pushed up through the upper line's loop / the symmetrical knot formed will CAPSIZE, or change shape, when the lines are pulled to snug it up.

A modification of the bowline, it is a quick, fairly secure bend.

47

the end is brought
back across, and then
under the lead

the end is passed
through the upper
loop of the "figure~8"

the knot is faired
and snugged up
toward the end of the line.

the FIGURE-EIGHT KNOT
is a quick, simple, workable
stopper.

stopper knot ▲ PREVENTS AN END FROM PASSING THROUGH A HOLE

binding knot WRAPS, SECURES, AND CLOSES ▼

the REEF KNOT, sometimes called the Square
Knot, is useful for binding and securing.

One end is passed
over and around the
other, and is snugged.

the same end passes
over and around
going the other way.

snugged, a strong
symmetrical binding
knot is formed.

* Danger *
the reef knot should never
be used as a bend (to tie
one line to another)~ it will give.

the SLIPPED REEF KNOT is used when the
object to be secured may have to be quickly
released, such as a furled sail.

it is begun exactly as
a reef knot, one end
over and around the
other.

a loop is made of that
end, and the loop is
taken back over and
around.

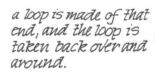

the knot is snugged
with the loop inside it.
yank the loop's end and
the knot will open easily.

the CONSTRICTOR KNOT will not slip
and holds like a vise, but it will not be
easily untied.

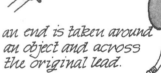

an end is taken around
an object and across
the original lead.

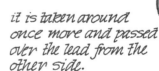

it is taken around
once more and passed
over the lead from the
other side.

now it is taken under
the crossing, and
snugged as tight as
necessary

coiling

Line at rest must be coiled and secured, or a sailing craft can become a hopeless tangle. It is important that the coils be made consistently, so that a new mate or a sailor fumbling in the dark is able to release them immediately. Accordingly, almost all sailors coil clockwise, and secure in one of a few methods.

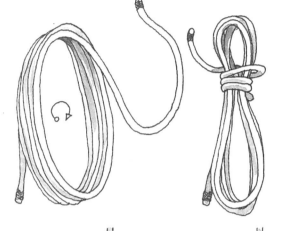

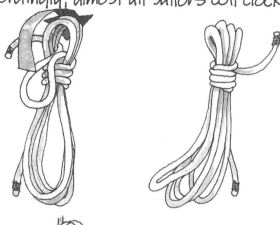

the body of the coil is wrapped three times, bottom to top / a loop of the wrapping line is stuck through the coil, between the sides / the loop is flipped over and around the top of the coil / the end of the wrapping line is snugged to secure the binding.

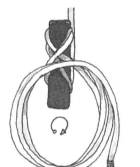

reach through the clockwise coil and pull back the loop of line nearest the cleat / twist the loop two or three times / jam the top of the twisted loop over the cleat's upper horn.

heaving knot

when a line is to be thrown, a careful, even coil is made / one end is secured to dock or boat, or put under the thrower's foot / a heaving knot may be tied in the throwing end / half the coil is held in the left hand, half in the right, with a dropped coil between to allow for a hefty swing / when one coil is thrown, it strips the remaining coil as it goes

Navigation:
the chart and compass

Navigation is knowing where you are and where you are going. On the land and in familiar surroundings, navigation is seldom difficult: our routes are laid out by streets and sidewalks, roadsigns and fences. Distances are marked or remembered from one particular tree or building to another landmark. Our way has been made clear. On the flat surface of the water, however, there are no trees, few markers, One wave looks very much like another and distances are incredibly deceiving. Not only does the surface provide little direction, but it masks the irregular terrain of the bottom, it hides shoals and rocks that reach up toward the bottoms of boats to catch and tear them. One of the lessons that sailing teaches is that safety often depends on an accurate sense of place~ a knowledge of exactly where you are, in safe water or running onto the hidden shoals. A sailor has two strong allies against the dangers under the surface: a chart and his compass. ~ It is not enough to say that a chart is a bird's eye picture, because it is so much better and more useful than a picture. A chart does not show just what APPEARS, but what IS. A chart shows submerged rocks, bars and shoals, channels, true directions, numbers of buoys and the flashing light codes of beacons, the shape of the bottom, and landmarks along the coast. Once you accustom yourself to the symbols and the system of nautical charts, you will begin to "read" the water easily and naturally. It will help you to get a chart of an area you know well, and to identify things you know with the chart's indications. Chart number 1210 Tr will help, a training chart with all its symbols and abbreviations explained, or the chart office's booklet of chart symbols.

"6"
GONG

These few pages cannot teach you the intricate art of coastwise navigation, but they may acquaint you with what the fisherman refer to as "eyeball navigation," an intimate familiarity with chart and compass that develops with use from a rough skill into an accurate craft.

50

some chart symbols

The symbols and indications on a chart tell the navigator what kind of buoy or object he can look for to estimate his position. These are only a few of the most common symbols. There are a hundred others, some as distant and adventurous as the marks and dangers Blackbeard's sailmaster looked for: coral reefs, windmills, Shinto shrines, forts, lava flows, glaciers.....and submerged wrecks.

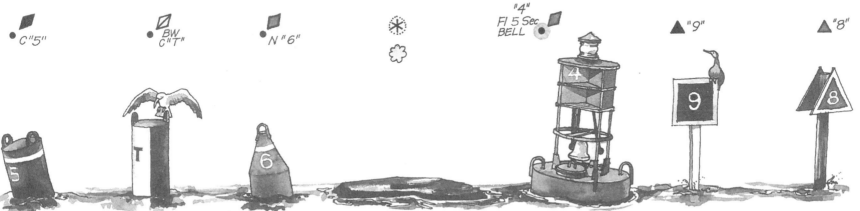

RED RIGHT RETURNING is a rule to remember, meaning that red buoys are on the right-hand side when entering a smaller body of water or a harbour. They are usually conical buoys called NUNS, and are marked with even numbers (2,4,6,8...). Black cylindrical buoys called CANS, marked with odd numbers (1,3,5,7...), mark the left side. Mid-channel buoys are black and white and lettered (A,B,C,D...). The symbol is a dot and a diamond, "C" or "N" for "can" or "nun."

Black asterisks mark rocks. If an outcropping of rocks is uncovered at low tide, it may be green on the chart with an uneven outline.

A violet circle around the dot for this diamond indicates a lighted buoy. No color is indicated, so the light is white, flashing every five seconds. This also has a bell for fog, but some have a whistle or gong.

Daymarks are set on stationary poles or pilings. Red triangles indicate red triangular marks with white reflective paint. Black triangles indicate square black marks with green reflective paint.

These are landmark position indicators along the shore, good marks to navigate by: a standpipe, a spire (there are several symbols for churches and steeples), a cupola, a tank, a smokestack, and a radio tower with its call letters and its tuning.

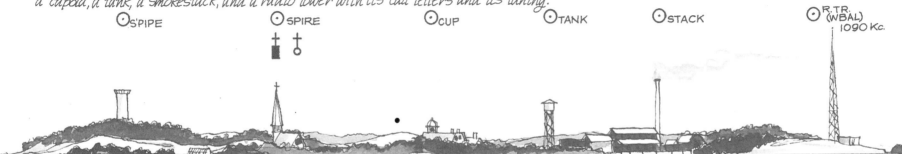

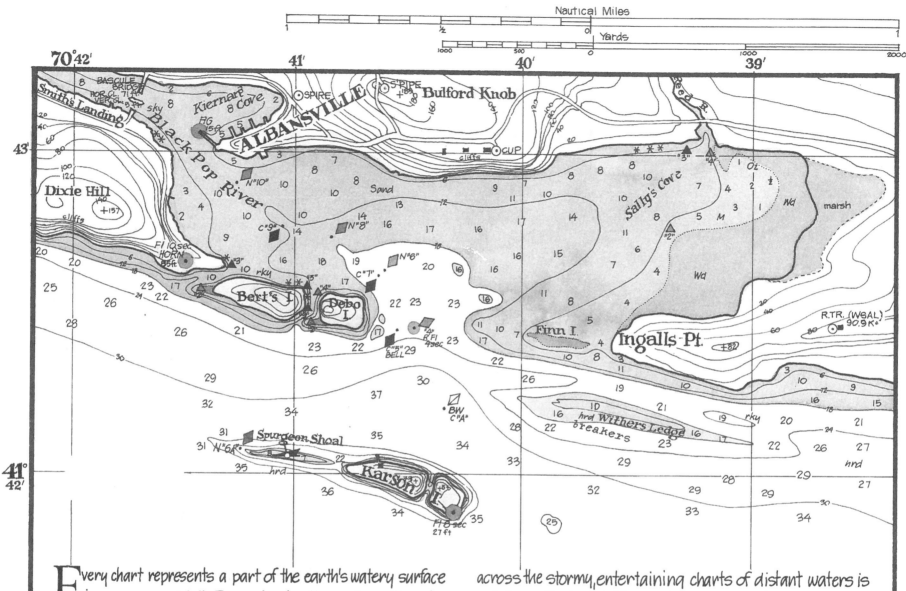

Every chart represents a part of the earth's watery surface in neccesary detail. Beyond a chart's exactness, though, there is a romance in the placement of things, in the course of streams surging past towns and opening to the sea, in the changing nature of the coast, and in the queer and fanciful names of coves, islands, and stretches of water. Armchair navigation across the stormy, entertaining charts of distant waters is a winter sailor's delight. ❧ The *soundings* (depths) are in feet, made at average low tide. Bottom shallower than 18 feet is tinted blue, the land is yellow. Ground which uncovers at low tide (like mudflats and marshes at the east end of the harbour, and Finn Island) are green. Deep, safe water is white.

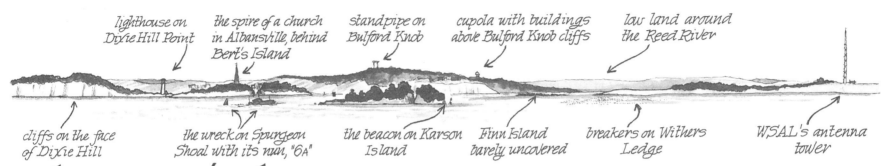

lighthouse on
Dixie Hill Point

the spire of a church
in Albansville, behind
Bert's Island

standpipe on
Bulford Knob

cupola with buildings
above Bulford Knob cliffs

low land around
the Reed River

cliffs on the face
of Dixie Hill

the wreck on Spurgeon
Shoal with its nun, "6A"

the beacon on Karson
Island

Finn Island
barely uncovered

breakers on Withers
Ledge

WSAL's antenna
tower

what is/what appears

Which is more real, the chart or the water? There is no wind in the chart; the birds do not cry from between its folds; the paper lays flat without the heave of waves. Then is the water more real? What you see on the surface and in the distance is only part of the whole; dangers and helps are concealed, the way to safety can be obscured by the haze of distance or the confusion of night. The appearance of things and the chart together make reality. 👓 In this view of the coast covered by the chart, there are several visual keys that stand out to give the navigator a sense of position. The buoys of the channel can guide a navigator into the harbour, if he keeps the red buoys on his right, and if the wind direction allows him to sail inside the channel without tacking. The chart, however, must tell him where he can leave the channel, where it is safe to sail. ~ The chart tells you that Albansville Harbour is fine sailing water. If your boat's draft is less than three feet,

it will safely sail within 100 yards of Bulford Knob Cliffs and as far east as Ingalls Point and daymarkers "2" and "4". Finn Island, since it uncovers, should be given a wide berth. The rocks on the northeast side of Bert's Island, on Dixie Hill Point, and to the west of the Reed River must be avoided. The water in the hollow of Dixie Hill, off the Black Pop River, is shallow and should be sailed cautiously. The chart shows that the passage between Bert's Island and Debo Island, though marked and passable, is not so wide and open as the passage between Bert's Island and Dixie Hill Point, which is not apparent in the view of the coast above. 👓 A small boat skipper should have charts of his sailing area near him for instant referral, to check depths, rocks, and the numbers of buoys. Charts are usually folded rather than rolled so they stay flat and can be held open in one hand

wreck symbol

the compass

Before the compass, sailing out of land's sight was a danger all sailors dreaded. Night and fog and clouds promised equal terror, for a navigator had no reliable directions but the sun and the stars on the featureless surface of the awesome sea. The Vikings sometimes carried crows in cages, freeing them to follow their flight homeward. ❧ Though the small boat sailor may not make long offshore passages, his compass is still primary equipment. When he understands it, it will give him honest directions, help him find his position, show him home. ❧ Simply, the compass points in one direction; the magnets in it align themselves with the earth's magnetic field, so the compass points near north. When you are using a compass, remember that there are three "norths." ✶ *True North* is the direction of the North Pole, the geometric top of the world. The system of position reference navigators use,(latitude and longitude) is based on True North. The vertical lines on your chart are lines of longitude, the lines of latitude are horizontal. ⚓ *Magnetic North* differs from True North because the magnetic field of the earth doesn't coincide exactly with its geometric directions. The earth itself is like a great magnet, but a slightly off-center, irregular one, so that the direction of Magnetic North changes from one part of the world to another. ⚜ *Compass North* is the north your own compass indicates, probably different from both True and Magnetic directions. It is important for you to know how much your compass differs from Magnetic North. Have an experienced navigator help you check it. It will be helpful to read the compass section in Chapman's *Piloting and Small Boat Seamanship* for more information about the compass and how it works. ❧ The needle of a landsman's compass turns within its ring of degrees, but a sailor's compass swings its whole degree ring past a stationary needle. The turning ring is called the *card*, the needle is called the *Lubber's line*. As the boat turns, the card remains oriented toward Magnetic North and directions, called *bearings*, are read by the lubber's line, which indicates the course or direction of the boat. Directions can be given in points (north, north – northeast, northeast, etc.), or more commonly in degrees (045°, 180°, 312°, etc.). ❧ In more than one place on your chart, you will find a *compass rose*, a double circle of directions in degrees, 000° to 360°. The outside circle indicates directions relative to True North, and may be of little help to small boat navigators who deal only in magnetic readings, indicated by the inner circle of degrees. The compass rose is a reference to all directions on the chart, and it is used with one of several tools designed to project a parallel line.

MAGNETIC

VAR 14°45'W (1964)
ANNUAL INCREASE 2'

Perhaps a sailor might want the bearing of the black entrance can to Albansville Harbour (C"5", BELL) from the nun off Spurgeon Shoal (N"6A"). Take a long, round pencil without an eraser, and place one edge over a line between the dots of the symbols. Now roll the pencil across the rose until one edge is over the mark at the center, follow the edge out to the magnetic degrees and read the bearing. It ought to be 069° M. (magnetic). Fishermen use a brass rod to do the same thing. The traditional navigator's tool is the parallel rule, which he "walks" across the chart, leg by leg. A clear vinyl sheet ruled with parallel lines is quick and fairly accurate. Some sailors find a mapreading compass like the Silva Ranger quick and handy. Many skippers draw a line along frequently run courses on their charts and mark them with the course bearings in both directions, and with the distance in nautical miles. Common dividers or the single-hand dividers are used to scale off distances. 🐌

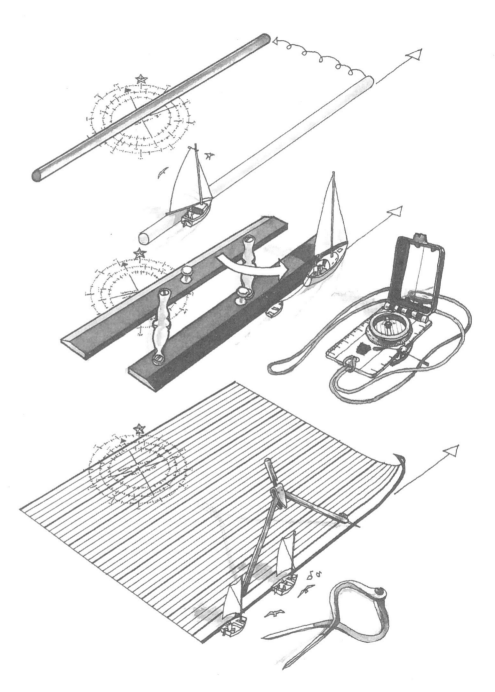

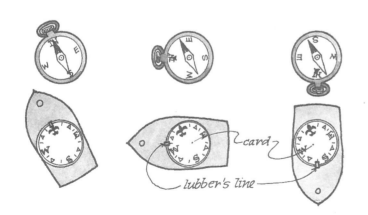

card

lubber's line

When a car traveling along Frambes Street reaches the intersection of Waldeck Avenue, its driver certainly has a sense of his position: he is at the intersection of two known lines. The navigator plots his position in the same way: he places his boat at the intersection of two (or more) lines of sight which he can locate on his chart. The sloop uppermost at right is at the crossing of two lines: a line through the nun and the can at the left, and between another nun and the tip of an island at the right. He knows where he is. The compass gives the navigator another invisible line: the three sailboats at the right are all on one line running through the lighthouse and the daymarker, but their compass courses to the nun place them at different points on the line. The double-ended boat below them is on a compass course for the lighthouse—one line—and when the pier is directly abeam, it has another line of reference. The boat traveling between the lighthouse and pier is taking soundings with a lead line (page 64) to use the depth lines as lines of reference.

position finding

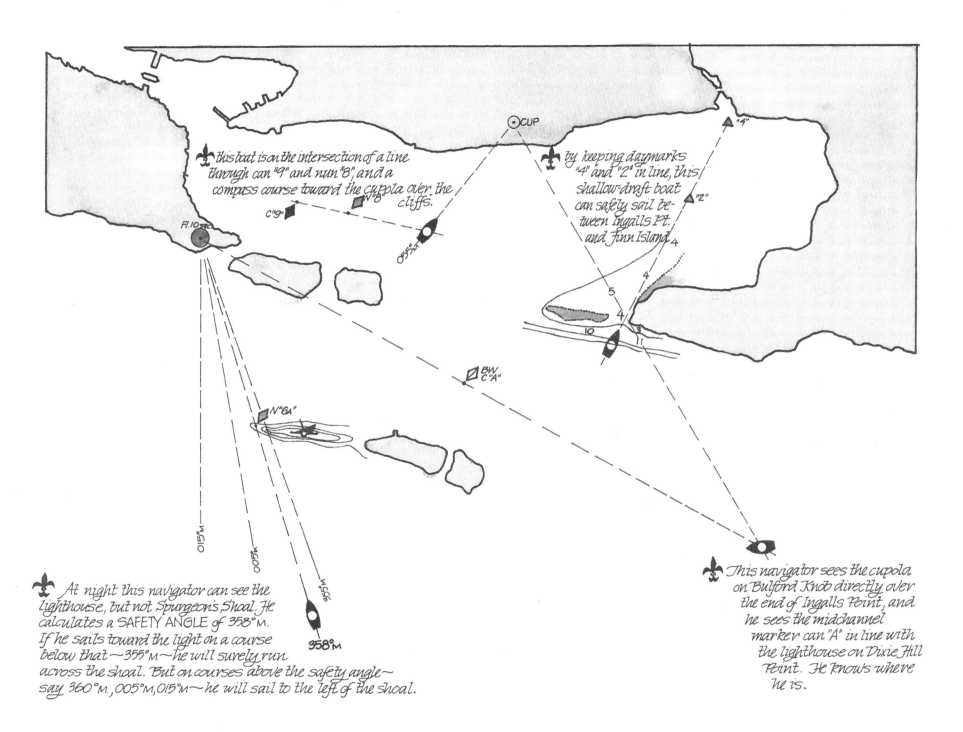

This boat is on the intersection of a line through can "9" and nun "8", and a compass course toward the cupola over the cliffs.

C"9" N"8"

055°M

⊙CUP

by keeping daymarks "4" and "2" in line, this shallow-draft boat can safely sail between Ingalls Pt. and Finn Island.

"4"

"2"

Fl.10 sec.

4

4

5

4

10 3

11

BW C"A"

N"6A"

015°M

005°M

355°M

358°M

At night this navigator can see the lighthouse, but not Spurgeon's Shoal. He calculates a SAFETY ANGLE of 358°M. If he sails toward the light on a course below that—355°M—he will surely run across the shoal. But on courses above the safety angle— say 360°M., 005°M, 015°M— he will sail to the left of the shoal.

This navigator sees the cupola on Bulford Knob directly over the end of Ingalls Point, and he sees the midchannel marker can "A" in line with the lighthouse on Dixie Hill Point. He knows where he is.

57

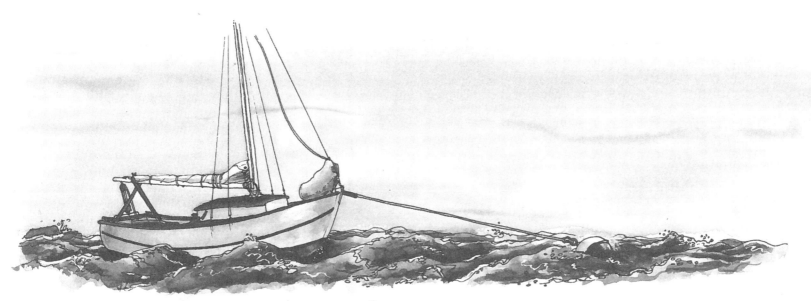

weather

Weather is all of sailing, from beginning to end, because a sailboat is wholly dependant on the weather over its water. The skipper of any boat–especially a small boat–chooses his weather; decides when and if he will sail, and his decision is a telling part of his seamanship. A skipper today is fortunate to have excellent weather reports available from commercial broadcasts or VHF continuous broadcasts (162.55 Mh, with stations at many locations along the coast), and he should never drop his mooring pendant without a good idea of what the weather will be. Since pharaoh Snofru's barges ferried his goods along the shore of Egypt, good skippers have always been cautious skippers. ⚓ A part of the coastwise sailor's daily weather is the state of the tide. Your chart and position-finding skills can tell you the general depths you are passing over, if you know whether the tide is high, low, flooding or ebbing. A passage impossible at low tide may be safe when the high tide floods four more feet of water over it. Keep the state of the tide fixed in your head each sailing day, and note the days of the higher spring tides each month. Remember that very high tides mean very low tides six hours away. Remember, too, that the moving tide causes currents that run more slowly or swiftly as the tide ebbs and flows, and that the currents are stronger as the greater tides occur. Consult a chart of the currents in your area, and plan your voyages to take advantage of the tidal currents as did the sailing masters of the canvas days. Try to leave with the current and return with it. ⚓ When a sailor has bad dreams, they are of storms, the sound of breakers, and fog. No sailor loves a storm, and he will avoid it any way he can, preferring a snug harbour to unkind wind and waves. The sound of breakers at night means that he has let his boat stray too close to a dangerous shore. Perhaps the worst dream, though, is the blank dread of the fog, denying the navigator all his lines of sight, obscuring all dangers, hiding the safe way home. If there is a possibility of fog, the skipper must stay near familiar territory and run for his mooring at the hint of an approaching fogbank. If he is to be caught in the fog, he should find his position on the chart as accurately as he can, for once surrounded, he will have only his chart, compass, watch, and his ears. In the fog he must know and trust his compass, and he must use (but mistrust) his ears. Listen. Listen for bell-and gong-buoys, for breakers, for foghorns and other boats. The fog plays tricks with sound, though, and you may not hear a nearby gong, or you may hear a distant foghorn as if it were very close. Put a radar reflector or a bag or metal foil high in the rigging to avoid collision with large boats. Sound your fog signal on horn or bell. (See below). Keep out of shipping channels. Making soundings with a lead-line may aid your navigation. Whether to anchor in untravelled water to wait out the fog, or to creep from buoy to buoy back into harbour is a decision the skipper must make, based on the circumstances and an appraisal of his own navigation skills. Keep in mind, though, that there is no shame in waiting out any question-able weather : the old sea-savvy skippers spent half of their time waiting for fair currents and fine winds

fog

St'b'd TACK	1 HORN BLAST/Min.	**Port** TACK	2 HORN BLASTS/Min.
Ring	3 HORN BLASTS/Min.	**Anchor**	5sec.BELL each Min.

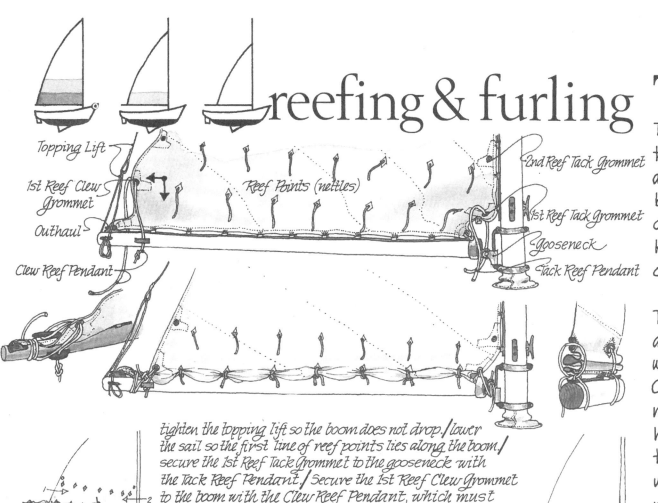

reefing & furling

Topping Lift

1st Reef Clew Grommet

Outhaul

Clew Reef Pendant

Reef Points (nettles)

2nd Reef Tack Grommet

1st Reef Tack Grommet

Gooseneck

Tack Reef Pendant

2 reef lines can be secured at the ends and laced through to knot at the middle.

tighten the topping lift so the boom does not drop./lower the sail so the first line of reef points lies along the boom./ secure the 1st Reef Tack Grommet to the gooseneck with the Tack Reef Pendant./ Secure the 1st Reef Clew Grommet to the boom with the Clew Reef Pendant, which must pull aft as well as down to keep the foot of the sail tight./ the reef points on either side of the sail are joined between the foot of the sail and the boom with a reef knot, taking care to place equal tension on all of the points./ hoist up the sail and slack the topping lift./

roller-reefing

Furling a sail secures it on the boom when not in use./SAIL STOPS (lines or cloth webbing to hold the sails) are hung over the boom under the foot of the sail/grasp a fold of the sail two or three feet from the boom and hold it near the boom to form a trough./the rest of the sail is stuffed into the trough and the trough is rolled over it/stops go over sail, under boom, are knotted over sail with a slipped reef knot.

The length of a boat's hull at its water-line determines its greatest speed. Though some racing sailcraft are designed to lift partly out of the water (to *plane*) and overcome this obstacle, most sail-boats are limited to an ultimate speed, called *hull speed*. The hull speed in knots is equal to 1⅓ the square root of the length at the waterline.

$$H.S. (k.) = 1⅓ \sqrt{w.l.}$$

Thus, a boat with a 16' waterline has an ultimate speed of 5⅓ knots, a 25' waterline has a hull speed of 6⅔ k. Carrying more sail than neccesary to reach hull speed only makes the boat heel more and become more difficult to handle. In even moderately strong winds, then, a small boat is safer, more obedient, and more comfortable if her sail area is reduced. The sail is made smaller by *reefing* it, bunching or rolling a section of the sail at its foot. Reefing is a useful skill that should become a normal practice when the wind rises. Furling can also be a high-wind skill, securing some sails aboard a multi-sail vessel to reduce the canvas area.

A boat under motor power must give way to a boat powered by the wind alone. / Exceptions: government vessels, any boat in a narrow channel, vessels too large to maneuver easily.

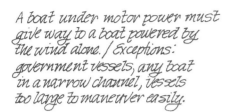

A boat running before the wind must give way to a boat working into the wind.

-rules·of·the·road

When yielding to another boat, change course sharply to show your intentions, and remember that he may not know the rules.

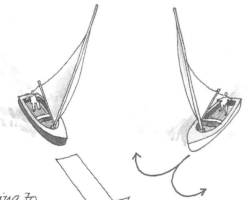

Two boats going to windward: the boat with the wind on its port side (port tack) must give way to the boat on starboard tack.

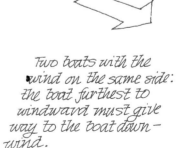

Two boats with the wind on the same side: the boat furthest to windward must give way to the boat down-wind.

61

anchoring

Perhaps the reason that the anchor is used in so many nautical symbols is that, to the sailor, the anchor means security and the end of a voyage. Anchoring is a critical part of your security, in harbour at rest and as a last resort measure if essential rigging or a sail is carried away. As a piece of emergency equipment, your anchor should not be stowed away, but immediately available for an unusual situation that threatens your craft. ❧ Anchoring is not just throwing a bottom hook over the side. Like all sailing maneuvers, it begins in the skipper's mind long before it happens. Before he enters harbour he is choosing his anchor (most cruising boats carry more than one anchor) and his anchoring ground from the chart. Thinking ahead to the weather and to how the wind will shift, he looks for shelter from wind and waves, away from channels. He looks for the notations of solid holding bottom: no anchor holds very well in a weedy or rocky bottom. The skipper chooses his depth, too. Perhaps a skipper entering Albansville Harbour might plan to anchor in the cove behind Dixie Hill, off the Black Pop River channel, believing that a southwest wind will prevail all night and he will be protected. The tide chart tells him that he is arriving at three hours after a normal low tide, and that the tide rise at Albansville is four feet. If he wants to anchor with at least six feet of water below him at low tide, he sails toward the shore with his anchor ready, taking *Soundings* with the lead line (below, right) until he reaches a depth of eight feet (six feet plus half the tide rise of four feet). ❧ *Anchor Rode* is the line and/or chain attached to the anchor. An anchor's *scope* is the relationship between the depth and the length

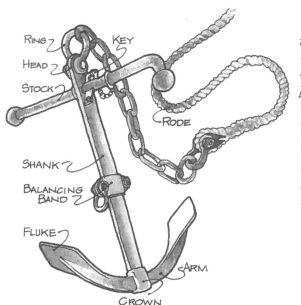

RING
KEY
HEAD
STOCK
RODE
SHANK
BALANCING BAND
FLUKE
ARM
CROWN

the Fisherman's, Yachtsman's, and the Herreshoff anchors are all similar to this pattern. It is an old design, but still unexcelled for use over a wide variety of bottoms. When winds and currents shift, however, the rode may foul around the fluke that is not stuck in the bottom ⤙

the Danforth pattern is popular, and indeed, it has tremendous holding power in sand or clay bottoms, but it can twist out with a shift, and will hold very poorly in weed or grass ⤙

the Plough Anchor holds well on good bottom, and is especially resistant to fouling and current/wind shifts ⤙

of the rode. A safe scope for a Danforth anchor is said to be 7 to 1, seven feet of rode for each foot of depth. Anchoring in a place where the maximum depth (at high tide) will be 10 feet, the skipper will pay out 70 feet of rode. If the wind rises, he will pay out even more line, because an anchor's holding power is much affected by the angle of the rode — the shallower the angle, the greater the holding power; and a longer rode gives a shallower angle (see below). Sailing into anchoring ground, the skipper may have a mate on the bow with the anchor and the correct length of rode ready. He might also cleat the rode, at its proper length, to the samson post, lead it through the bow chock and back to the cockpit <u>outside</u> the shrouds — in this way the anchor can be dropped from the cockpit in a moment. The boat will be brought into the wind, and when its motion stops, the anchor will be carefully dropped overside so the rode will not wrap around the stock or flukes on the way down. The boat drifts back and the rode is paid out. The weight of the boat and windage of the sails should set the anchor into the bottom (powerboats reverse their engines to set their anchor/s). Even after an anchor is set and holding, a good skipper (always cautious) keeps track of his position to make sure his boat is not slipping. He can do this by taking bearings or establishing lines of reference to objects ashore. He will check his anchor through the night in case a wind shift has twisted his anchor out or has fouled it with its own rode and pulled it out. Skippers sleep lightly aboard an anchored vessel

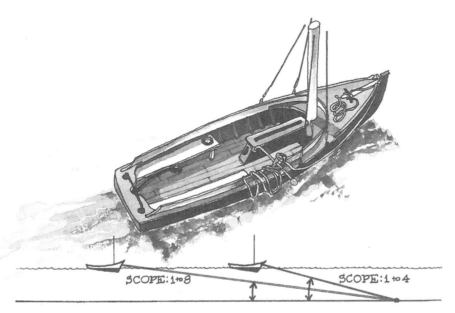

SCOPE: 1 to 8   SCOPE: 1 to 4

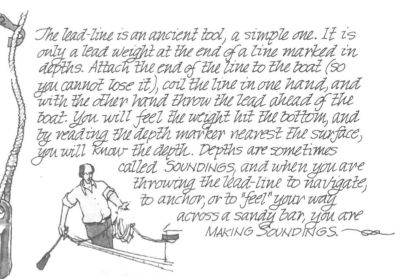

The lead-line is an ancient tool, a simple one. It is only a lead weight at the end of a line marked in depths. Attach the end of the line to the boat (so you cannot lose it), coil the line in one hand, and with the other hand throw the lead ahead of the boat. You will feel the weight hit the bottom, and by reading the depth marker nearest the surface, you will know the depth. Depths are sometimes called SOUNDINGS, and when you are throwing the lead-line to navigate, to anchor, or to "feel" your way across a sandy bar, you are MAKING SOUNDINGS.

Many of a boat's parts are named on page 25 ⟶ ☜

index